# LIA COOK

## MATERIAL ALLUSIONS

INEZ BROOKS-MYERS

Curator of Costume and Textiles

OAKLAND MUSEUM OF CALIFORNIA

Library of Congress Catalog Card Number: 95-69810

ISBN: 1-882140-08-7

Oakland Museum of California
Art Department
1000 Oak Street
Oakland, California 94607-4892

Catalogue design by Gordon Chun Design, Berkeley, California

Printed in Hong Kong through Overseas Printing, San Francisco, California

INSIDE COVERS, PAGE 18:
Detail of *Loin Cloth Series: Anonymous,* 1995

# CONTENTS

# FOREWORD

The San Francisco Bay Area and, more specifically, Berkeley and the East Bay have long been highly regarded in artistic circles for their contributions to the textile and fiber arts. The University of California, Berkeley, Department of Design, with respected artist-teachers such as Ed Rossbach, and the California College of Arts and Crafts, Textile Department, in Oakland, have for decades provided a matrix for experimentation and innovation in the field. Lia Cook ranks high among the many accomplished artists making up this fertile scene.

The Oakland Museum of California has enjoyed a close association with these artists, collecting and exhibiting their work and providing a public forum for their ideas. This exhibition, *Lia Cook: Material Allusions,* is the most recent in a succession of projects exploring the achievements of the artists of our time and place.

On behalf of the Oakland Museum of California, I want to thank Inez Brooks-Myers, Curator of Costume and Textiles, for her service as curator and project director for this important undertaking. We are grateful to Lia Cook for the active role she maintained throughout every phase of this exhibition. Finally, I want to express appreciation to the many lenders to the exhibition for generously sharing works from their collections, and to the National Endowment for the Arts, the California Arts Council, and the Friends of Fiber Art International for their essential support of this exhibition and its accompanying publication.

PHILIP E. LINHARES
Chief Curator of Art

# ACKNOWLEDGMENTS

The exhibition *Lia Cook: Material Allusions* has been in preparation for over two years. We have enjoyed the full cooperation of the artist, Lia Cook, and her dealer, Louise Allrich, of the Allrich Gallery, San Francisco. Without them, for obvious reasons, this project would not have been possible. Our debt to them is beyond words.

Staff members of the Oakland Museum of California worked outside the limits of their jobs to make this exhibition and catalogue realities from which we can all benefit. Phil Mumma, Deputy Director for Public Programs, and Philip E. Linhares, Chief Curator of Art, have supported the idea for this exhibition from the start. Janice Capecci, Kaoru Kitagawa, Arthur Monroe, Karen Nelson, and Patrice Wagner dispatched their responsibilities with their usual efficiency. Kathy L. Borgogno, Curatorial Aide, managed the myriad details of planning and scheduling that go into projects of this scope. She was helped by the catalogue's editor, Fronia W. Simpson, who guided us through the labyrinth of words created to accompany works of art. None of this would have happened without Jerry Daviee, of the Development Department, who wrote successful grant applications to the National Endowment for the Arts and the California Arts Council. Judy Wood and the Art Guild have offered help on many fronts.

A thank-you to all those who helped fund the exhibition: The National Endowment for the Arts, the California Arts Council, *FIBERARTS / The Magazine of Textiles,* Camille Cook and the Friends of Fiber Art International, and the Members of the Oakland Museum of California.

The Oakland Museum of California is grateful for the work of all these people, and many not named here, and is proud to present the exhibition *Lia Cook: Material Allusions.*

INEZ BROOKS-MYERS
Curator of Costume and Textiles

# INTRODUCTION

*Inez Brooks-Myers*

CURATOR OF COSTUME AND TEXTILES

In this catalogue, Matthew Kangas, writer on art, shares his view of Lia Cook's work as it relates to ancient, traditional, and industrialized European textile techniques. He uses the mythology of ancient Crete, the textile history of the Renaissance, and the family history of the artist to give us a perspective on Cook's work.

Chelsea Miller Goin looks at the textiles of Lia Cook from the perspective of an anthropologist and social historian. She discusses Cook's work in relationship to textiles as metaphors for the female experience in art and everyday life. Miller Goin also makes us aware of Cook's theme of textiles as medium and subject matter in both her early work and her more recent pieces.

Finally, the scholar Janis Jefferies examines the artist's work specifically inspired by the old masters. Approaching her subject from a feminist position, while acknowledging the sensual quality of the work, Jefferies discusses how the art of Lia Cook visually illuminates the semiotic theories of Julia Kristeva.

The strength and symbolism of the work of Lia Cook will never be overshadowed by the physical, lyrical beauty of her textiles. But there is a message; the focus is on textiles, and the "medium is the message." On the other hand, we should not shy away from our appreciation of beauty, especially in the work of Lia Cook.

Lia Cook's work has always aroused the emotions and received praise. As early as 1978 the renowned art critic Alfred Frankenstein lauded her work in the *San Francisco Chronicle:* "Lia Cook works in wool, cotton, silk and doubtless in other fibers as well. She does all manner of exceptional things with her hangings. . . . However the effect is attained, it is always extremely beautiful. If fiberworks hadn't already won their place as a valid art form, Lia Cook would achieve that victory single-handedly."

# LIA COOK

## ARIADNE IN BERKELEY

*Matthew Kangas*

FOR MARY RAJALA KANGAS, WHO SPUN HER OWN WOOL (1880–1962)

## INTRODUCTION

Now, before Daedalus left Crete, he had given Ariadne a magic ball of thread, and instructed her how to enter and leave the Labyrinth. She must open the entrance door and tie the loose end of the thread to the lintel; the ball would roll along, diminishing as it went and making, with devious turns and twists, for the innermost recess where the Minotaur was lodged. This ball Ariadne gave to Theseus and instructed him to follow it until he reached the sleeping monster, whom he must seize by the hair and sacrifice to Poseidon.[1]

Although certain materials (abaca, a banana fiber), techniques (thread painted prior to weaving), and processes (layering of images) are Asian influences in the art of Lia Cook, a European, and specifically Mediterranean, context for her work has been overlooked. This essay attempts to provide that context briefly and to discuss a body of work made since 1982, which culminates in works that underscore the California artist's great achievements: expanding the limits of textile-art traditions; confounding medium-specific critics by combining painting and weaving; attaining a profile and influence in Western Europe that put her on a level with few other American textile artists; and creating a subtle, complex, and richly varied series of weavings which radiate ambiguous yet satisfying levels of meaning.

A product of the American craft revolution of the 1960s, specifically the fiber-art movement in the San Francisco Bay Area, Lia Cook is a major artist so prolific that this exhibition alone cannot encompass all her shifts, transitions, and evolutions in style. Nevertheless, it is the purpose of this essay, and of the contributions by the curator, Inez Brooks-Myers, and coauthors, Chelsea Miller Goin and Janis Jefferies, to create a context for understanding, appreciating, and enjoying Cook's art.

Like Ariadne, daughter of King Minos on the Greek island of Crete, Cook has used thread (or yarn) as line, as unraveler of meaning, as basic tool for an elaborate path toward artistic realization which, as in the mythical labyrinth, has often crossed back on itself only to lead eventually to a new starting point or opening into the light of day. Whether cotton, rayon, or abaca fiber, it has undergirded the images and reinforced the themes of Cook's art.

What are those themes, those strands of meaning, which have emerged over a twenty-year period? First, the tug-of-war between two- and three-dimensional art is one continuum that affects image, form, and content. Next, physicality, sensuality, and tactility are toyed with, exploited, and investigated again and again through the creation of the woven and painted object.

These lead to the realms of the veiled, the concealed, the mysterious—and the erotic. As a curtain may be lifted and dropped at will to reveal theatrical events, so Cook plays with the image of the drapery or curtain as a symbol of display and presentation. Although the curtain is usually the forerunner of event, in

1

Cook it becomes the event. This introduces the themes of edge, marginality, and detail, which are moved to the forefront. By seizing on the detail of a drapery in an old-master painting by Leonardo, Dürer, or Artemisia Gentileschi, Cook moves the marginal to the center, thereby reversing a long-standing prejudice in Western art: the literal edging out of textiles. In a brilliant post-modern strategy, Cook centralizes the neglected, rescuing the "minor" arts of decoration, subverting the conventional wisdom that craft or decorative art cannot contain or express deep content.

Finally, devotion bordering on the ecstatic or spiritual is another key theme. Related to process and construction, the laboriously slow and precisely elaborate technical aspects of Cook's woven works are not a central part of this essay, but the attendant devotion involved in their execution is an important path to their understanding. This devotion is the result of her expressive response to materials on both an emotional and an intellectual level. The intertwining (worthy of Ariadne) of complicated structure and image is the result of an absorption, a hardheadedness, which may only be described as devotion.

With her paternal grandfather's family coming from a village near Pordenone in northern Italy, Lia Cook gravitated to an interest in historic Italian textiles and the handmade in general. Artisanship is also a part of her European heritage; her paternal grandfather, Luigi Polese, built furniture according to his own designs. In addition, the satisfaction of complicated problem solving came naturally to the daughter of James Polese, who invented types of electronic tubes.[2] The combination of problem-solving powers and a craftsman's abilities made Cook a likely candidate for picking up the thread of textile arts which so flourished in Europe from the fourteenth through the seventeenth centuries.

Eventually, she was led to conduct extensive research at, among other places, the Henry Art Gallery at the University of Washington in Seattle, where she examined samples of cut and uncut voided velvet woven in Italy between 1600 and 1635 (fig. 1), as well as earlier fragments of Spanish damask weaving. Looking

at them, her own interest in scale, repetition, and idiosyncratic abstract units of pattern was deeply reinforced. Confirming these links, recent Italian critics have commented on the analogies in her work to four centuries of tradition.[3]

And although her combination of Asian and European processes may seem jarring to some, it is important to remember that such a synthesis had already taken place in fifteenth- and sixteenth-century Italy: silk technology, original examples, and patterns from the Islamic world and China were the dominant factors in transforming European weaving and making possible the triumphs of Italian and French Renaissance tapestries.

Coming full circle, then, Cook's *New Master Draperies* (begun in 1991) and the *Material Pleasures* series (begun in 1993) make cultural and historical references to both medieval and Renaissance Italy, its textiles and paintings, its accomplishments, which, like Cook's, face both East and West.

Fig. 1. *Cut and uncut voided velvet (fragment), Italy, c. 1615–35. 9⅛ x 6½ in. Henry Art Gallery, University of Washington, Gift from the Art Institute of Chicago, 63.9-9.*

A perfect rag-bag of odds and ends . . . the whole assortment shall be lightly stitched together by a single thread. . . .

—Virginia Woolf, *Orlando* (1928)

Just as Virginia Woolf's heroine spanned centuries weaving a variety of attire "stitched together by a single thread," so Cook developed her art through a combination of historical awareness and attention to the contemporary moment, all connected by Ariadne's ancient thread. Her studies with Ed Rossbach at the University of California, Berkeley, in the early 1970s grounded her in both the history of textile traditions and the possibilities of what textile art could become. Her own tribute to Rossbach (written for his 1990 retrospective catalogue at the Textile Museum in Washington, D.C.) carefully analyzed the influence of this quiet yet towering figure in American craft. Cook's formal and informal sessions with the Cranbrook-trained teacher reinforced her sense of individual vision rather than any predetermined professorial direction: "Doing anything in reaction to Rossbach was difficult because you never knew where you stood. I never knew exactly what he thought. Yet not knowing suited my way of working quite well. I became my own critic."[4]

All the same, one can see traces of Rossbach's art in Cook's—and vice versa. His use of photographic imagery, such as the one appearing in his *Handgun* (1975), may have led to Cook's taste for a subliminal image. In return, his *Damask Waterfall* (1977) shares the same shape—square—and weave structure as much of Cook's work. Although Cook shied away from Rossbach's Pop art imagery, she agreed with many of his other freewheeling attitudes toward textiles, such as the idea that the artist will find the right material for the right idea regardless of its humble or unexpected source. Cook's 1967 weaving studies at Handarbetets Vänner, in Stockholm, were the original inspiration to commit her life to textiles, but, again, it was Rossbach who was the experimental, Americanizing influence on

this artist so aware of European traditions.

Her frequent inclusion in museum exhibitions in Switzerland, the Netherlands, Germany, Spain, Norway, and Belgium attests to her perhaps greater reputation abroad than in the United States, and her three important solo exhibitions—in Oslo (1993), Liège (1989), and, most significantly, in Beauvais (1983), the spiritual nerve center of French tapestries—confirm the interest in her work on the part of European curators and dealers. The Beauvais retrospective at the Galerie Nationale de la Tapisserie et d'Art Textile was widely attended, enthusiastically reviewed, and accompanied by an extensive catalogue essay by Rémy Prin, which reproduced all Cook's major works to date.[5]

*Rope* (1974) and *Coming Through* (1978) remind us of the actual three-dimensional pieces which would later become spatial illusions. Relating to much postminimalist sculpture of the day, like the work of Eva Hesse and Robert Morris, *Rope* defies a monumentality of form, as does *Bedroom Fantasy* (1974), and offers instead a sequential linear shrinking of sculptural volume without recourse to the blocky, somber masses of Minimalism.

Within the year, Cook had gone even farther, flattening the surface and imprinting it with photographic images of ropes rather than the real shape of rope previously constructed (*Knot,* 1974). Her work became at once more conceptual and more material oriented—or craftlike. With the simulacrum of a three-dimensional object—a rope—twining its way across a bulging surface, Cook next addressed ways of heightening the tactile qualities of the surface. Here concept was sacrificed for physicality, and many works of the late 1970s were filled with polyurethane foam, or the surface itself was turned into an object through folding and twisting the heavy woven forms.

Recalling topographical maps, other undulating works like the *Landforms* series (1978) alternately alluded back to Optical-Perceptual art or forward to the Pattern and Decoration movement. Elsewhere, in *One and Twenty* (1978) and *Two Point Four* (1980), the grid predominated as image, both accentuating the

3

basic structure of weaving and playfully violating or altering it by setting up contrasting lines or poles, which implied a shallow pictorial space reminiscent of Cubism.[6] Growing in size, Cook's weavings before 1982 constitute her earliest phase of maturity.

The basic themes of interplay between two and three dimensions; the rich tactility of the textile surface and its limitless possibilities; and the introduction of a mysterious, ambiguous picture plane are all laid out with cautious power and assured artistry. Armed with the confidence of the Beauvais retrospective, she refined the body of work featured in the current exhibition.

## LIFTING THE VEIL

Draped forms appearing from and disappearing, into the darkness . . .

—Lia Cook[7]

Although the first use of the drapery or curtain image appeared in *Fabric I* and *Fabric II* (1982), it was not fully explored for a few years. *Hanging Net* (plate 3) literalizes the fold again, this time using the wall as a support, as in *Rope.* It is typical of how Cook's art interplays volume and flatness, object and image. It also foreshadowed Cook's most important works to date, the weavings in various series that use the image of a folded drapery or curtain emerging from a pressed abaca, rayon, or linen surface. Not only that, it was a harbinger of her large-scale museum installations using both flat drapery-image panels and real draped fabric.

Before those explorations began in depth, however, a trip to the People's Republic of China in 1984 had a different kind of impact. A pilgrimage to Mecca for any textile enthusiast, this sojourn in the land where silk and the fine textile tradition of Asia began resulted in Cook's excursion into the "imperial" style. *China Stage Curtain, China Curtain II,* and *Through the Curtain and Up from the Sea* (plate 4) were all completed upon her return. Using repeated scallop-shape modules, each describes a graduated vertical "landscape" evocative of

the abrupt frontality of Chinese landscape painting, executed without recourse to Renaissance perspective. The curves are repeated in the top and bottom edges of each "curtain," accentuating an illusion of billowing fabric. Colors are rich as well, restricted to tones of red, yellow, and blue, all subtly and sumptuously modulated. Cook's pressing of the weaving once it is off the loom also mimics the effect of Chinese couched embroidery, another province of imperial style.

*Dolly's Crazy Quilt* (plate 5), *Crazy Quilt: Royal Remnants* (plate 6), and *Framed and Draped: Material History* (plate 7) all share a broad palette and deep modeling. By now, Cook has added a border to each and settled on a repeated triangular motif common to American folk-art quilts. Besides intersecting irregular polygons in *Dolly's Crazy Quilt,* a swooping white grid or net pattern sways in the upper right-hand corner. (The work is inspired by a prize-winning quilt made by her great-grandmother, Dolly Boyes Hopkins, in the artist's collection.) This motion is repeated in *Royal Remnants,* using a "royal blue" area extending across the upper half. Rather than lifting the veil, the veil or fabric image is the central figure. Among Cook's most visually complicated works, the series reaches a culmination in *Leonardo's Quilt* (plate 11), which, again, lifts pattern modules from fifteenth- and sixteenth-century Italian textile samples. Brighter, more reflective, this work's jagged diagonal movement animates the surface, drawing further attention to Cook's "material history," her postmodern invocation of prior traditions. In addition, she mixes the purported "high" and "low" cultural traditions of oil painting and folk-art quilts.

Switching to the banana fiber, abaca, in *Oil Cloth* (1988) allowed Cook a more supple painting surface after washing, shrinking, and pressing the weaving. This gave full rein to her interest in painting. As she told the Women's Caucus for the Arts in Chicago in 1992: "I enjoy the irony of using the established 'masters' . . . to confront our assumptions about the hierarchies of subject matter, media, and other materials."

It is my opinion that discussion of the precise sources for the images in the *New Master Draperies* and

*Material Pleasures* has somewhat obscured analysis of the individual works. What matters more (and what will be evident to viewers of this exhibition) is the way Cook has set tight chromatic limits for herself (a base of red-pink and blue-green) and mined them deeply within each approach. The color choice mimics black-and-white photographic reproductions in art-history books, further distancing us from the originals and pointing out details of famous paintings: the role of textile as prop, appurtenance, afterthought.

Cook is moving the marginal to the center, lifting the veil on textile history, and expressing devotion to the European heritage of court weaving while critiquing painters—and art historians—who have downgraded cloth's significance as a result of rigid academic conventions.

At first, in *Oil Cloth*, *Sashay*, and *Shadow Frieze* (plate 10), the curtain was given full play, approximating a covered window. In *Shadow Frieze,* the drapery is accentuated in three groupings stretching to a width of nearly six feet.

With *Leonardo III* (plate 13), *Leonardo IV* (plate 14), and *Michelangelo* (plate 12), the *New Master Draperies* series shifts toward greater surface-and-shadow contrast with less emphasis on symmetry. Glaring light sources seem just offstage, highlighting folds that may or may not cover anatomy or furniture. Varying the pattern module from piece to piece (triangles, lozenges, diamonds), Cook invokes the Mediterranean textile masterpieces as well as the painters to whom the weavings are dedicated. *Florentine Fresco* (plate 20), with its single towellike form, is especially successful in this sense because its left- and right-leaning patterns seem directly inspired by the Italian originals. With less chromatic variation and a blunt frontal placing of the towel, Cook's strategy of appropriation and devotion emerges most clearly.

A major installation at the Museum Van Bommel-Van Dam in Venlo, the Netherlands, in 1993 returned Cook to the interplay of object and image which is at the heart of her oeuvre. *Material Pleasures* included *Dürer, Giulio R., Leonardo III,* and *Artemisia* from the series (see plates 22–24), positioning them on the wall between bunched sections of computer-woven Jacquard fabric designed by Cook and made especially for the installation, while she was artist-in-residence at the Müller-Zell Company in Zell, Germany, near Nuremberg.

With the weavings displayed Salon-style, Cook created her own museum setting, lifting the veil on the overlooked, drawing back the curtain to reveal her responses to art history, old and new weaving techniques, all filtered through a creative imagination of extraordinary breadth. There was another purpose as well. The panels act as windows on an erotic panorama of the body. Fabric is used in relation to human anatomy, a new direction Cook continues today.

In conclusion, the art of Lia Cook builds on the heritage of European culture but has done so through a subjective vision of that culture, elevating the personal and expressive to a level of meaning with subtlety and skill. Combining illusion with a paradoxical material presence, she has challenged the way we perceive and encounter the real world. Along with other major American craft artists of our time, Lia Cook has restored the independence of beauty and its relevance in an art of complexity, nuance, and significance.

## NOTES

1. Robert Graves, *The Greek Myths* (Harmondsworth: Penguin Books, 1955), vol. 1, p. 339.

2. Lia Cook, in conversation with author, July 19, 1994.

3. "Stilisti de oggi/Lia Cook/Tessuti come opere d'arte," *Jacquard* (June 1990): 14–15; Esperienze Didattiche, "Il corso sulle tecniche dei tessuti operati, Fondazione Arte della Seta Lisio," *Jacquard* (September 1990).

4. Lia Cook, "Ed Rossbach as Educator: A Personal View," in *Ed Rossbach: 40 Years of Exploration and Innovation in Fiber Art,* ed. Ann Pollard Rowe and Rebecca A. T. Stevens (Asheville, N.C.: Lark Books; Washington, D.C.: The Textile Museum, 1990), p. 100.

5. Rémy Prin, *Lia Cook: Identités textiles,* no. 2 (Beauvais: Galerie Nationale de la Tapisserie et d'Art Textile, 1983).

6. Nancy A. Corwin, *Lia Cook* (Washington, D.C.: National Academy of Sciences, 1990).

7. Lia Cook, unpublished statement for the panel discussion "Materiality and Content," Women's Caucus for the Arts, Chicago, 1992.

# THE TECHNOLOGICAL STYLE OF LIA COOK

*Chelsea Miller Goin*

There are many art histories. In the humanities and social sciences, art has always played a significant role in the study of culture. Currently, psychologists, archaeologists, anthropologists, and sociologists are challenging Euro-Western concepts of art and establishing new perspectives for the history(s) of art. Through biological and cognitive research and cross-cultural perspectives, social scientists are reconceptualizing "art" itself, discovering it as a primary influence on human behavior, as a critical element in establishing social organization and as a vital factor in the system of production that constitutes the material basis of society.

From an anthropological point of view, art and artistic expression are not autonomous domains[1]—the making of art is a form of human behavior that occurs within a sociocultural matrix. Culture, beliefs, feelings, rules, and expressions around which people organize their lives and societies constitute the environment in which art is conceived and produced. An anthropological study of art is holistic in that it examines the art process within the complex entirety of culture: the specific biological, environmental, technological, and historical contexts of culture, the social role and gender of the artist, and the intricate web of relationships between artistic expression and social life.

The study of textiles lends itself well to an anthropological approach, for textile history is the story of human history. As a cross-cultural, historically continuous technology, textiles have expressed and symbolized ritual exchange, social and political power, and ideological and aesthetic values. When fabricated into clothing, textiles have symbolized gender, identity, class, occupation, rank, membership, or affiliation.[2] Textile history incorporates the history of technology from the "string revolution" of prehistory to the invention of spindles and horizontal and vertical looms, through the numerous inventions for textile production in the industrial revolution, including the Jacquard loom.[3] With its punch cards and unique binary system, the Jacquard loom was used as a model for the development of the first digital computer. The commodification of cloth is synonymous with economic and political developments from the Silk Road developed after Marco Polo's journeys, to the changing role of cloth during the French Revolution, to modern trade sanctions. Textile history also incorporates linguistics. Within the English language, textile processes, technology, and commodities have played a seminal and historical role in our concepts of organization, structure, and community.

Eurocentric class hierarchies, reflected in the stratification of the arts into "fine arts," "folk and primitive arts," "industrial arts," and "crafts," have separated art and expressive behavior from their primary bases within culture. The histories of these forms are separated as well, assembling the arts of painting, sculpture, architecture, and highly decorated ceramics into one history, while separate histories are established for crafts (which include metallurgy and jewelry, pottery, and textiles, basketry, and costume), design, and even photography. Textile history establishes a postmodern approach in analyzing textiles as material culture. This approach combines cross-cultural theories about the nature of "art," examines the technological development, sociocultural practice, and aesthetic expression of a medium within a historical context.

The art of Lia Cook is conceived, constructed, and expressed through the history and language of textiles. The symbolic meaning of Cook's work is best determined by examining it from an anthropological, rather than a strictly art-historical, point of view. Cultural interpretations of textiles as artifacts, as crafts, and as art have an underlying theme. All three ideologies are based on the premise that textiles are "women's work." How textiles are perceived, ranked, and function within a cultural framework is structured by this engendering process. By briefly reviewing aspects of the prehistoric and historic records, by examining the diachronic linguistic expressions of textile production, and by redefining the concept of weaving as both a technical and a philosophical process, the work of Lia Cook can be examined from a dynamic new perspective.

## TEXTILES AS TECHNOLOGIES

Loosely defined, the word *fabric,* from the Latin *fabricare,* "to build," "to fabricate," is a generic term for constructions of fiber.[4] The term *textile* generally refers to woven fabrics, but baskets and mats, as woven structures, are included under the textile rubric.[5] Cordage has multiple references but here specifically refers to the plying or doubling of plant fibers. Thus, textiles are constructions of organic materials, materials that decay and frequently leave no traces.

In the archaeological record, non-loom weaving predates ceramics, metallurgy, and agriculture and is earlier than writing.[6] Recent excavations at an ancient village in the Sea of Galilee in Israel have yielded fragments of twisted plant fibers 19,300 years old. Scientists have identified these fibers as the earliest known examples of human textiles.[7] A Paleolithic "Venus" figure carved in stone was depicted wearing a one-sided string "skirt" of twisted cordage. The figure, found in a cave near Lespugue, France, dates to 20,000 years ago.[8] In the Lascaux caves in southern France, an imprint of a twisted cord made of plant fiber was discovered in the cave floor and has been dated to 15,000 B.C. Structurally sophisticated loom-woven textiles, from well before 6000 B.C., have been discovered in the Middle East at Catal Huyuk and Nahal Hemar. Egyptian textile production was a critical part of the Egyptian economy by 4500 B.C.[9] In the New World, textiles also show great antiquity. Rabbit-fur blankets dating to 8000 B.C. and twined baskets and sandals dating to 9000 B.C. have been discovered in the dry desert caves of the Great Basin in Nevada and sections of Utah, Idaho, Oregon, and Southern California.[10]

Textile technology is abundant in the prehistoric archaeological record. Evidence of textile structures, such as those cited above, and their implied existence and use in associated artifacts such as bone or antler needles or harpoons,[11] demonstrate that textile technology and production made important and possibly critical contributions in prehistoric cultures.[12] The fact that research on stone-tool manufacturing and hunting weapons is extensive while research on net making and cordage is only limited raises questions of gender bias. The implication is that stone tools and hunting are male-related technologies, while textile technologies are associated with women, though there is no archaeological evidence to support this view. Current research in archaeological theory points out that even when cordage was not implicitly allied with female-related technology, it was generalized as being linked with the female domain and therefore devalued as an activity.[13] Our concepts of the present are predicated on our interpretations of the past.

## WHY ARE TEXTILES CONSIDERED "WOMEN'S WORK"?

Scholars have assumed that working with fibers to produce textile structures has been a feminine activity, beginning with early prehistory and continuing to the present. However, the evidence for this association is ambiguous and misrepresentational. Textile technologies have been considered "women's work" based on economic strategies that divide labor into male and female domains. Men's technologies have been seen to be those associated with hunting and geographically wide-ranging activities, while women's technologies have been associated with those closer to a home base. Judith Brown and Patty Jo Watson with Mary Kennedy point out that, universally, women have the primary responsibility for raising children and at the same time perform extensive subsistence work.[14] Repetitive activities that can be done successfully without focused concentration are interruptable and are thus best suited for those with child-care responsibilities. Researchers, classifying textile technologies under this general description, have labeled all such activity "women's work." However, Conkey argues that those who used the tools were primarily (but not exclusively) responsible for making and maintaining them.[15] Thus, cordage used on harpoons and spears or threads used in binding or sewing tools would be considered male concerns. Schneider points out that in early modern Europe, division of labor was at a minimum, since everyone, men, women, and children, labored on the crops and spun.[16] Arterburn illustrates that domestic responsibilities and weaving are not compatible; the loss of a domestic household member from weaving activities is almost always connected with child care and not with domestic activities such as cooking and cleaning.[17] Infants and small children must be closely supervised to keep them away from the looms, where they might distract the weaver or damage the materials and equipment.

When the vertical loom was introduced in Egypt, textile production became the province of men. When cloth was produced for sale outside the home, or when industry came in as new, prestigious, or profitable, Egyptian weavers were male.[18] Wesley Thompson establishes the dichotomy that in early Greece women produced clothes for use by the family but men manufactured cloth for sale in the market. Quoting Plato's *Republic* and Aristotle, Thompson argues that weaving, as a commercial enterprise, was man's work.[19] In her study of silk-weaving cooperatives in Kanchipuram, India, Arterburn notes that adult males work full time at weaving and adult females also work full time, assisting their husbands at the loom.[20] If women have small children they prepare the weft yarns for weaving and tend to domestic chores. In Mexico and Latin America, women continue to dominate the indigenous backstrap loom while men confine themselves to production weaving on the European-introduced floor loom.

With the advent of the industrial revolution, cloth production became more strictly engendered—within the domestic sphere textiles were feminized and cloth manufacture solely for economic gain or commerce became culturally associated with male domains (as in the Egyptian and New World examples). And yet, if we look at the images by the early-twentieth-century documentary photographer Lewis Hine, we see that a large percentage of the factory workers were *not* men, as might be anticipated, but women and children.[21] More ethnographic studies and research in textile production in prehistory and within domestic and product-oriented economies need to be done to understand more clearly divisions of labor and the rubric "women's work."

Again, why are textiles considered women's work? While the answers to this question deserve a larger forum and deeper analysis, the fact remains that the work of Lia Cook and many other contemporary textile artists has been marginalized by critics, curators, galleries, and museums because of engendered and socially stratified cultural hierarchies. Despite textiles' central historical role in the production of culture, they have virtually been eliminated from modern art history. The postmodern rejection of modernism and feminist critique in the 1980s of the androcentric biases in art history and anthropology have forced a reevaluation of cloth's role in economics, semiotics, diachronics, and aesthetics.[22] Linguistic analysis, examining how we speak about textiles and their production, is a fundamental method for establishing a new point of view.

Throughout Western traditions, textile processes and fabrication have been used as metaphors. In *Cloth and Human Experience* Annette Weiner recalls Homer's description of Penelope, weaving Laertes' shroud by day but unraveling the same fabric each night, thereby seeking to halt time. The European folktale of Rumpelstiltskin, who spun straw into gold, is a weaver's alchemic tale, while the story of Sleeping Beauty uses the spinning wheel as a transformative device.[23]

Today, in expressing fundamental concepts of social wholeness, we say "the fabric of society," "the cloth of human experience," or "they're a closely knit family," and even postmodern approaches such as material culture employ a textile metaphor to describe the interdisciplinary research in art history, anthropology, archaeology, cultural geography, folklore, and antiquities.

Threads are conceptualized as connective elements—the "threads of discourse," "his life was hanging by a thread," "she's stringing him along," or the new term for computer-information systems, "Internet." Weaving, spinning, knitting, quilting, and netmaking are constructive integrative acts, joining disparate elements into a new whole—"she fabricated a model" or "he mended his ways." During the 1988 presidential campaign, a candidate appearing on national television used the quilt as a metaphor for healing and bringing the party, and the nation, into wholeness. And we use textile metaphors to express disintegration or disorder—"her life unraveled," "after the divorce she picked up the threads of her life," "postwar remnants," "he's tied up in knots," and "we must reweave the tattered cloth of society."

Etymologies are important as well. The word *text,* from the Latin *texere,* means "to construct" or "to weave," and, as stated earlier, the root of the word *fabric* refers to construction. The word *loom,* as a noun, is derived from the Old Norse *hummr,* "the handle of an oar" and/or from the Old English *geloma,* meaning "tool." Yet as an intransitive verb, *loom* refers to the appearance or coming into clear sight of a person or object, especially above the surface of the sea or land, referring to the process of cloth production when the fabric begins to appear on the beam. An *heirloom,* once a specific piece of equipment to be passed on, now generically means all property viewed by the law as an inseparable part of an inheritance.

Textile terminology is also frequently duplicitous. The phrase "he was a spinner of yarns" doubles as "he was a teller of tales." The word *distaff* refers to the rod that holds raw linen for spinning or to women's work and the female gender, "the distaff side." In this instance the distaff rod, as equipment for transforming raw material into a finished product, becomes an analogue for feminine reproductive activity. The word *spinster* can be used to define a person's occupation or trade yet more frequently describes the productive, rather than reproductive, capabilities of an unmarried woman. These examples all illustrate that the metaphorical nature of textiles is commonplace in our language, but why is this important?

The discovery of the rich linguistic heritage of textile terminology and metaphors in our contemporary language establishes a historical continuity of relevance and meaning, despite extreme social, cultural, and technological change. While the social role of textile production has changed radically in the last two thousand years, many of our primary concepts of social relationships are based in the language of textile processes.

Metaphors are concepts for action. Although metaphors are characteristically thought of as existing only in language, recent work in linguistics has shown that our conceptual system, in terms of which we both think and act, is fundamentally metaphorical in nature.[24] Our concepts structure what we perceive, and they play a central role in defining our everyday realities. A method to analyze these concepts is to look at language. Since communication is based on the same conceptual system that we use in thinking and acting, language is an important source of evidence for what that system is like.[25] The abundance of textile metaphors in our language demonstrates that textile processes and their resulting structures and products are not merely objective knowledge but subjective knowledge as well. Textile techniques and constructions are deeply rooted in our concepts and manifestations of part-to-whole relationships, social organization, and community. Textile metaphors fabricate our reality.

## WEAVING IS AN EPISTEMOLOGY

A review of early textile production and textile metaphors is critical because it illustrates that weaving is not simply a technical procedure but functions additionally as a conceptual framework. Every textile, whether it is a "simple" linear cord, a two-dimensional mat, or a three-dimensional basket, plain-weave cotton cloth, or the complex computerized multiharness structures of Lia Cook, requires objective *and* subjective knowledge. Objective knowledge is familiarity with materials, refinement of techniques, and a comprehensive understanding of architecture. Subjective knowledge is the conceptual formulation of design, combining ideas about purpose, function, aesthetics, and meaning in the abstract realm.[26] Through craft or praxis, both forms of knowledge integrate into a single system. As a system of knowledge, textiles play a significant role in the reproduction of culture. If we conceptualize individual and social relationships as "woven," "fabricated," "bound," "knit," or "unraveled," we reproduce them in our language and actions. Weaving is an epistemology.[27]

As a conceptual framework and performative act, weaving can be understood in cognitive and visceral terms. The epistemology of touch describes knowledge generated by our senses[28]—what we "know" through touch, sight, and sound rather than through strictly cognitive processes—our intuitive grasp of things. Weavers know through the act of touch when fiber is properly or improperly spun, when threads are calculated at the proper tension and sett (number of warp threads per inch), when a fabric has the right "hand." Qualities of smoothness are determined, not by calibration but by touch. Dye mordants can be "measured" through their aromas. Color is evaluated, not through its wave length on the spectrum but through our visual perception of it:

when a blue warp has red wefts we see the fabric as purple. And our senses work in tandem with our cognitive knowledge: we see purple where a weaver or painter, trained to see color in its component parts, would see particles of red and blue. The qualitative aspects of what feels or looks "right," like the draping of cloth on the body or in space—are judged through visual and tactile, as well as aesthetic, criteria. The anthropologist Clifford Geertz affirms the notion of the epistemology of touch when he writes:

> If there is any commonality among all the arts in all the places that one finds them . . . it is not that they appeal to some universal sense of beauty. . . . If there is a commonality it lies in the fact that certain activities everywhere seem specifically to demonstrate that ideas are visible, audible, and one needs to make up a new word here—tactible, that they can be cast in forms where the sense, and through the senses the emotions, can reflectively address them.[29]

The epistemology of touch emphasizes that knowledge, constructed of cognitive and sensate information and realized through praxis, is holistic.

## THE TECHNOLOGICAL STYLE OF LIA COOK

The art of Lia Cook combines the representation and aesthetics of fine art with the technology and epistemology of craft. Cook emphasizes that in her work, "Fabric is both the subject matter and the material object in itself."[30] Utilizing sources from the histories of art and cloth production, Cook's research incorporates a variety of materials, including historic fabric samples from European and American museums, renderings of draperies and cloth in Renaissance and historic paintings, the operation and maintenance of a Jacquard loom, an Apple computer with a diagrammatic weaving program, and a variety of papers, drawing tools, paints, and varnishes.

In the initial phase of her work Cook diagrams complex multiharness patterns, then weaves them into cloth. The patterns constructed within the cloth act as a two-dimensional skeleton onto which she builds representational or abstract images. The potentials or limitations of the structure and materials, the "architectural constraints" of the canvas,[31] guide, but do not predict, the forms. The resulting style of Cook's work is a composite of concepts, techniques, materials, and images, or "technological style."[32] The tools, techniques, and materials selected by Cook not only express her ideas but also reflect cultural concepts regarding these technologies. Such a technological style is based on the premise that concepts and emotions are expressed through the techniques and materials used. An analysis of the production process in conjunction with the stylistic analysis of imagery can provide a wider scope of meaning.

Cook's quilts and draperies are not simply illustrations of textiles. What the images are *of* and what they are *about* operate on different levels.[33] Cook's images, from the early "cloth over landscape formations" to the towels, curtains, and more recent quilts and draperies, are images of cloth painted on highly patterned canvas. The textile images, however, are about the cultural issues and hierarchies of subject matter within Euro-Western art history and the contemporary art world. The draperies and quilts act as referents or symbols for the conceptual framework of weaving (structure, order, process, and performance), for the rich patterns and sources of textile history, and for the engendered domain of cloth production.

Cook's work must be interpreted from a structural, as well as from an aesthetic, point of view. For Cook, weaving is symbolic[34] and is *the* conceptual framework that orders her ideas and establishes her processes. Structure is not extrinsic but intrinsic in her work. When Cook selects an image of interlacing elements she uses it as a visual metaphor for the concepts "primary" or "fundamental." It is from this, she implies, that everything else evolves. When she selects a complex patterned weave, frequently based on a specific historic textile, Cook is directly referring to the social, political, and historical uses of cloth. Weaving processes and pat-

terns provide a foundation for the structure of the cloth as well as for its meaning.

Cook's weavings are made of a variety of natural and man-made materials—abaca, linen, and rayon as well as acrylic paints and polymers, which are submitted to a series of processes. One method involves weaving a patterned cloth, immersing it in water, and flattening it by running it through a press. The cloth has become a canvas on which the artist paints. After the imagery is completed, the pieces are backed with stiffened industrial canvas for strength and portability. The multiple processes and techniques clearly establish Cook's postmodern methodology, in which she combines the architectural concepts of weaving and the color theories of painting, without notions of hierarchy, all of which express an overlay of historical concepts about cloth.

The pictorial representation of fabric and drapery has a long history. From the prehistoric Venus "skirt" to Greek vase painting and sculpture, to its associations with holiness and luxury in the European medieval period, to Renaissance renderings in painting and sculpture or its nineteenth-century use as a visual frame in heroic, political, or holy scenes, the representation of draped cloth symbolizes cultural ideals. Anne Hollander points out that the representation of draped cloth is an essential element of idealized vision, and that the "natural" beauty of cloth is a cultural construction.[35] Dick Hebdige affirms Hollander's notion that the representation of draped cloth, whether in clothing or interior architectural space, carries meaning beyond its literal depiction.[36]

Cloth as subject matter communicates on a number of levels. Within the domestic sphere, cloth is utilized in a variety of ways—as clothing, bedding, towels, and furnishings. These objects operate on two planes. First, they function in a direct manner to cover our bodies, maintain our warmth, allow us comfort and privacy. Second, they convey meanings and ideologies. Hebdige notes that all aspects of culture possess a semiotic value; a curtain is not just a curtain but conveys important ideological information.[37] Curtains, as an integral part of a domain, define space. In their flexibility they divide interior from exterior, activate light, and separate interior space, often signifying the gendered division of labor within that domain. The types of materials used and the actual style of the curtain itself carry connotations of conspicuous consumption or class hierarchies.

Cook's series the *New Master Draperies* draws on the drapery studies of Leonardo da Vinci and the old masters for inspiration. By recontextualizing the imagery, Cook creates a powerful and ironic statement regarding our assumptions about the hierarchies of subject matter, media, and gender issues. Her use of drapery over the human figure emphasizes the dichotomy of the function of cloth. Fabric, as a material object, operates as both a two-dimensional surface and a three-dimensional form. Cook plays with this duality—as a painting surface, as sculpture over a human form which both reveals and conceals that form, and as architecture when used to define space. Stanley Trachtenberg states that

> [t]he content of postmodernism is unabashedly ordinary for the most part, with a scope that seems to focus in a particularly unblinking and sometimes reportorial manner on all the various areas of the social and cultural fabric that threatens to unravel, as well as on those areas of deepest psychological stress. Far from novel, postmodernism in all of its variant strains seeks to return to its most primitive roots as a regenerative source of energy and understanding.[38]

In her structural concepts, choices of technology and materials, as well as visual style, Lia Cook integrates theory and practice into a refined system of knowledge. In her consistent themes of Euro-Western art hierarchies, historic interaction of cloth with the social system, and the cultural engenderment of cloth as a commodity and cloth as an art form, Cook's work speaks eloquently to the postmodern issues of contemporary society.

NOTES

I would like to thank Catherine Fowler, Norris Brock Johnson, and Fronia W. Simpson for their comments and review of this essay.

1. For more on the stratification of the arts see Henry Glassie, *The Spirit of Folk Art* (New York: Abrams, 1989), and *Turkish Traditional Art Today* (Bloomington: Indiana University Press, 1993); Margaret W. Conkey, "Humans as Materialists and Symbolists: Image Making in the Upper Paleolithic," in *The Origin and Evolution of Humans and Humanness,* ed. E. Tab Rasmussen (Boston: Jones and Bartlett, 1993); Ellen Dissanayake, *Homo Aestheticus* (New York: Macmillan/Free Press, 1992), pp. 194–202; Edward Lucie-Smith, "Historical Roots and Contemporary Perspective," in *Craft Today: Poetry of the Physical* (New York: American Craft Museum, 1986), p. 37; John Perreault, "Crafts Is Art: Notes on Crafts, on Art, on Criticism," in *The Eloquent Object,* ed. Marcia Manhart and Tom Manhart (Tulsa, Okla.: Philbrook Museum, 1987); and Chelsea Miller Goin, "Who Are the Folk in Folk Art?" n.d., unpublished paper.

2. Annette Weiner and Jane Schneider, eds., *Cloth and Human Experience* (Washington, D.C.: Smithsonian Institution Press, 1989).

3. Alice Marcoux, *Jacquard Textiles* (Providence: Rhode Island School of Design, 1982); E. J. W. Barber, *Women's Work: The First 20,000 Years* (New York: W. W. Norton, 1994).

4. Irene Emery, *The Primary Structure of Fabrics* (Washington, D.C.: The Textile Museum, 1980), pp. xvi, 8.

5. J. M. Adovasio, "Prehistoric Basketry," in *Handbook of North American Indians, Great Basin,* vol. 11 (Washington, D.C.: Smithsonian Institution Press, 1986), p. 194.

6. For more on the relationship of prehistoric textiles and the origins of agriculture see E. J. W. Barber, *Prehistoric Textiles* (Princeton, N.J.: Princeton University Press, 1991), pp. 10, 79; Barber, *Women's Work;* Kent V. Flannery, ed., *Guila Naquitz* (Orlando, Fla.: Academic Press, 1986); Jack Goody, *The Interface between the Oral and the Written* (Cambridge: Cambridge University Press, 1987), pp. 18, 24; Richard W. Redding, *A General Explanation of Subsistence Change: From Hunting and Gathering to Food Production* (Orlando, Fla.: Academic Press, 1988); David Rindos, "Symbiosis, Instability, and the Origins and Spread of Agriculture: A New Model," *Current Anthropology* 21, no. 6 (December 1980): 751–72; and Patty Jo Watson and Mary C. Kennedy, "The Development of Horticulture in the Eastern Woodlands of North America: Women's Role," in *Engendering Archaeology,* ed. Joan Gero and Margaret Conkey, Social Archaeology Series (Oxford: Basil Blackwell, 1991).

7. D. Nadel, A. Danin, E. Werker, T. Schick, M. E. Kislev, and K. Stewart, "19,000-Year-Old Twisted Fibers from Ohalo II," *Current Anthropology* 35, no. 4 (1994): 451–58.

8. Conkey, "Humans as Materialists," p. 97, points out that most interpretations of Paleolithic paintings, sculptures, and engravings do not include technologies as critical factors. She argues that the technology must be incorporated into any thorough analysis of art.

In her "Contexts of Action, Contexts of Power: Material Culture and Gender in the Magdalenian," in *Engendering Archaeology*, p. 76, Conkey describes the devaluation and deletion of textiles from the archaeological record.

9. Barber, *Prehistoric Textiles*, pp. 40–41.

10. Adovasio, "Prehistoric Basketry," p. 194.

11. Conkey, "Contexts of Action," p. 76.

12. Chelsea Miller Goin, "Textiles as Technologies in the Archaeological Record," in progress.

13. Conkey, "Contexts of Action," p. 76; Barber, *Prehistoric Textiles* and *Women's Work*.

14. Judith Brown, "A Note on the Division of Labor by Sex," *American Anthropologist* 72 (1970): 1073–78, and Watson and Kennedy, "The Development of Horticulture."

15. Conkey, "Contexts of Action," pp. 78–79.

16. Jane Schneider, "Rumpelstiltskin's Bargain: Folklore and the Merchant Capitalist Intensification of Linen Manufacture in Early Modern Europe," in Weiner and Schneider, *Cloth and Human Experience*, p. 187.

17. Yvonne J. Arterburn, *The Loom of Interdependence: The Silk Weaving Cooperatives in Kanchipuram* (Delhi: Hindustan Publishing Company, 1982), p. 35.

18. Barber, *Prehistoric Textiles*, pp. 290–91.

19. Wesley Thompson, "Weaving: A Man's Work," *Classical World* 75 (1982): 217–22.

20. Arterburn, *The Loom of Interdependence*, p. 35.

21. Steve Dunwell, *The Run of the Mill* (Boston: David Godine Publisher, 1977), and Alan Trachtenberg, *America and Lewis Hine, 1904–1940* (Millerton, N.Y.: Aperture, 1977).

22. Janet Catherine Berlo, "Beyond Bricolage: Women and Aesthetic Strategies in Latin American Textiles," in *Textile Traditions of MesoAmerica and the Andes: An Anthology*, ed. Margot Blum Schevill, Janet Catherine Berlo, and Edward D. Dwyer (New York: Garland Publishing, 1991), p. 438, and Suzi Gablik, *Has Modernism Failed?* (New York: Thames and Hudson, 1984), p. 119.

23. Chelsea Miller Goin, "A Poetry of Transformation," *Artweek* 18, no. 39 (November 21, 1987): 4.

24. George Lakoff and Mark Johnson, *Metaphors We Live By* (Chicago: University of Chicago Press, 1980), p. 3.

25. Lakoff and Johnson, *Metaphors*, p. 3.

26. Mark Johnson, *The Body in the Mind* (Chicago: University of Chicago Press, 1987), and Dissanayake, *Homo Aestheticus*, attempt to reintegrate the body-mind dualism held for centuries by philosophers in the Western tradition by arguing that knowledge has a biological base and cannot be separated from the body.

27. I am using the term *epistemology* after the fashion of Gregory Bateson (*Mind and Nature: A Necessary Unity* [New York: Bantam Books, 1979], pp. 4, 246). Bateson discusses epistemology simplistically as how we can know anything. From a scientific perspective, epistemology is the study of how organisms know, think, and decide. Philosophically, Bateson defines epistemology as "the study of the necessary limits and other characteristics of the processes of knowing, thinking and deciding."

28. Norris Brock Johnson, "Art and the Meaning of Things," *Reviews in Anthropology* 17 (1990): 221–34.

29. Clifford Geertz, "Art as a Cultural System," in *Modern Language Notes* (Baltimore, Md.: The Johns Hopkins University Press, 1976), p. 1499.

30. Statements by the artist are excerpted from "Materiality and Content," a panel discussion held at the Women's Caucus for the Arts, Chicago, 1992.

31. Stephen J. Gould and R. C. Lewontin, "The Spandrels of San Marcos and the Panglossian Paradigm: A Critique of the Adaptionist Programme," *Proceedings of the Royal Society of London* (1979): 581–98.

32. Conkey, "Humans as Materialists," p. 107.

33. For more on the literal and symbolic meaning of objects (semiotics) see Roland Barthes, *Mythologies* (New York: Hill and Wang, 1972), and Dick Hebdige, *Subculture: The Meaning of Style* (London: Routledge Press, 1979).

34. Jacques Maquet, *The Aesthetic Experience* (New Haven, Conn.: Yale University Press, 1986).

35. Anne Hollander, *Seeing through Clothes* (New York: Viking/Penguin Books, 1978), p. xii.

36. Hebdige, *Subculture*.

37. Hebdige, *Subculture*, p. 13.

38. Stanley Trachtenberg, *The Postmodern Movement: A Handbook of Contemporary Innovation in the Arts* (Westport, Conn.: Greenwood Press, 1985), pp. 66–67.

# Touching Material, Reading in Detail

*Janis Jefferies*

I have analyzed elsewhere how the discredited exclusions of Western art history—gendered subjectivity, the metaphorics of femininity, and the language of textiles—have permeated the painted signs of luxury and wealth, ownership and possession, as an obscene encounter between luscious folds, interior drapery, and commodity spectacle. But for whose display? For whose orgasmic delight?[1]

Lia Cook's *New Master Draperies* series reshapes this encounter by representing fabric (as a sign of interior drapery) as both subject matter and the material object of her textile practice. Her painted, dyed, and woven cloths deliberately embrace the imagery of drapery through an appropriation of the drapery studies of Leonardo da Vinci and other old masters. The finished cloths of Cook's draperies parody the established "masters" disguise. Her fabric forms and formulates new questions as to the hierarchies of subject matter, cultural value, and gendered subjectivity within the field of contemporary textiles. For me, her fabric studies magnify and repattern the expunged details of the old masters in ways that shift the meanings of the material object. This is a point to which I will return.

Cook's works invite me to enter a new perceptual field of inquiry in which sight is no more important than any other sense. As I cast my eyes over the six woven panels of *Drapery Frieze: After Leonardo* (plate 19), there is no prescribed viewing position. There is no fixed state of otherness as produced by the male gaze nor a celebration of the dominant scopic regime. The "mastery" of

the artist's eye and hand is displaced in much the same way as the fixed gaze of the monocular spectator is removed from the scene he once occupied and enjoyed.[2] What was once historically and culturally marginalized and devalued as a decorative extra (within the rigid confines of the regularly ordered space of the picture frame) erupts and transgresses the borders of containment. The seemingly insignificant and crumpled details of interior drapery are, in Lia Cook's work, magnified and celebrated as explicit material presences. Although a clearly defined body or figure is absent from my view in *Drapery Frieze: After Leonardo,* the shape and form of the draped cloth evoke a bodily presence that presses against the folds and veils of cloth in a metaphor for skin, a membrane that invites a closeness between the perceptual edges of the absent body and my own fleshy responses to the enclosing fabric.

This membrane is composed of colored particles of magnified detail. The detail, for me, returns in Lia Cook's work as the repressed signified; the place of the feminine as a site of preverbal tactile memories, which fuse the temporal rhythms of the material/maternal body.

To "read in detail"[3] is also to explore the language of proximity rather than distance, touch rather than sight, and the "economy of flow"[4] that "takes each figure back to its source, which is among other things tactile."[5] To scan over details of *Drapery Frieze: After Leonardo* is to be free to roam through the textured surfaces of material. I am made acutely aware of my mobile glance. This acknowledges the potential pleasures of corporeal desire, not as an orgasmic delight for the male gaze but as a recognition that my own vision is triggered by fleshy, sensuous experience and is inseparable from my body and its relations to the unconscious.[6]

I want to suggest that in Lia Cook's work this foregrounding of the culturally devalued detail operates as both sign and signified of the feminine, its association with textiles and gendered subjectivity. If I am seduced by these "new" luscious folds of drapery fabric it is because they allow me a place, as a female viewer, to exchange a "sensuality of touch, an implied caress," which has "no climactic place or moment."[7] Consequently, *Drapery Frieze:After Leonardo* becomes a counterpoint to the single, climactic moment of male consummation which operated inside and outside the picture frame. My reaction to Lia Cook's drapery images are therefore visceral. They offer me a number of reflexive viewing positions. I am continually invited to embrace the work from within a register of shifting subjectivities and bodily mobility, which conjures up a range of associative pleasures. These finished cloths have been reinscribed with the cultural significance of *écriture couverture* (as in the manner of a comforting bed quilt) and are, I believe, produced out of *écriture féminine,* a different body of experience for which there exists no rational language.[8] Could these experiences, coupled with my own, also be synonymous with "women's time"?[9]

In Lia Cook's work, draped forms appear and disappear, not into the lightness of ocular immediacy nor into the dark continent of femininity (as Freud would have "us" believe) but refer us to a place where Kristeva's psychoanalytic proposition of the *chora* may operate.[10] For Kristeva, the *chora* is the site of the undifferentiated bodily space that the mother and child share and which in part explains her notion of the semiotic. The semiotic is made up of nonsignifying raw materials and formless bodily impulses and energies. These have no fixed aim but enliven the child's body in a series of unconnected movements and sensations that have no fixed sexual orientation or position. They come before any conscious corporeal control. These impulses

and energies can be said to precede the distinction between object and subject and the child's comprehension of a thing as separate from itself. In this sense, the clearly marked boundaries between object and subject, the mother's and child's bodies, are blurred. It is here that I want to suggest that the semiotic becomes a sign of the repressed feminine, since that which is most marginalized in phallocentric culture is the text of her self, which is responsive to the mother's voice in pre-Oedipal development. According to Kristeva, the semiotic has to be given up in order that we may acquire a stable, social, or symbolic position as a unified male or female subject. This symbolic position has come to stand for the paternal and patriarchal laws of language, tied to the symbolic father and the castrated mother. The semiotic resists meaning and generates material/maternal pleasure, but it is assimilated and silenced by the symbolic. This silence and repression of the feminine is the condition and the price of civilization. But as feminist theory has so productively and creatively explored, the dominance of the symbolic is never stable or secure. In adult life, the semiotic, the maternal *chora,* can return via the sensation of bodily rhythms and mobile impulses at those precise and yet unsuspected moments of physical upheaval and at the juncture where the supposed coherent meaningfulness of cultural discourse breaks down. Here, as when I scan Lia Cook's work, the semiotic begins to threaten the boundaries of artistic practices and limits, the hierarchies of subject matter and meanings of the material object to the point of revolutionary rupture. As the expunged detail of the old masters overflows into the abundant pattern of *New Master Draperies,* so the "semiotic" maternal tongue of drives disrupts the "symbolic" language of signification.

I have often felt that Lia Cook's drapery images visually illuminate Kristeva's theories of the semiotic. Cook's work moves me to recall and re-remember the preverbal tactile memories that are evoked through the power of cloth, its rhythms, colors, and tones that wrap us to ourmothers' bodies. For although Kristeva describes the semiotic as feminine, it is not reducible to its intelligible, verbal translation. I may unravel some of the complex meanings that Lia Cook's work generates but I am left enraptured by the supplementary excesses of semiotic eruption, linguistic play, tactile sensuality, and material tangibility as I snuggle under the covers to a dream of bliss.

## NOTES

1. Janis Jefferies, "Text and Textiles: Weaving across the Borderlines," in *Towards Feminist Criticism: Into the 1990s,* ed. Katy Deepwell (Manchester University Press, forthcoming), pp. 164–73.

2. I am indebted to the critical scrutiny of vision by Martin Jay in *Downcast Eyes: The Denigration of Vision in Twentieth Century French Thought* (Berkeley: University of California Press, 1993), and his analysis of vision's allegedly superior capacity to provide access to the world of things and people. An ocularcentric discourse, as Jay points out, can be linked to phallocentrism, as is argued in the writings of Julia Kristeva, Hélène Cixous, and, most particularly, Luce Irigaray. Each has offered various claims for a woman's special relationship to language, which is frequently couched in antiocular terms. The temporal rhythms of the body, according to Jay's interpretation of Kristeva, Cixous, and Irigaray, rupture the mortifying spatialization of the masculine eye and, I believe, offer a useful model for rethinking the ethics of touch in relation to textiles.

3. Naomi Schor's *Reading in Detail: Aesthetic and the Feminine* (London: Methuen, 1987), opens up the story of the detail to analyze how it has been aligned with the feminine and how the patriarchal paradigm has historically held the detail in contempt. However, Schor argues that the detail makes a triumphant return, for example, in the writing of Proust and Barthes as an appropriation of the feminine.

4. Luce Irigaray, "Questions," in *This Sex Which Is Not One,* trans. Catherine Porter and Carolyn Burke (Ithaca, N.Y.: Cornell University Press, 1985), p. 148.

5. Irigaray, "The Power of Discourse," in ibid., p. 69.

6. Norman Bryson mounts a convincing argument for this reading in *Vision and Painting: The Logic of the Gaze* (London: Blackwell, 1983), p. 94, while Rosalind Krauss has interrogated the relationship between the body and the unconscious to suggest that vision is "carnally constituted." See Rosalind Krauss, "The Story of the Eye," *New Literary History* 1, no. 2 (Winter 1989): 283–97.

7. Rachel Blau DuPlessis, "For the Etruscans," in *The New Feminist Criticism: Essays on Women, Literature, and Theory,* ed. Elaine Showalter (London: Virago Press, 1986). This extraordinary essay is an excellent example, in my view, of the collage aesthetic, which combines autobiography, textual analysis, and a wide range of cultural material. This collage provides a place for mourning, a place for the female in, primarily, Western culture. As such, it may be analogous to strategies employed in quilt making to which Lia Cook's work also refers.

8. In "Piecing and Writing," Elaine Showalter appropriates the term *écriture féminine* to coin the phrase *écriture couverture* as a way of linking piecing, as in quilt making, with American women's writing during the nineteenth and twentieth centuries. See entry "Piecing and Writing," in Nancy K. Miller, *The Poetics of Gender* (New York: Columbia University Press, 1986), pp. 222–47. *Ecriture féminine* has been defined as experimental writing. Initially French, *écriture féminine* has been characterized as "writing the body" or "writing through the body," to provide an argument for a woman's language. Cixous and Irigaray's psychoanalytic writings can be particularly identified as being closer to the mother's voice and the flesh and rhythms of our earliest awareness of language. For a useful reading see *Feminism and Psychoanalysis: A Critical Dictionary,* ed. Elizabeth Wright (Oxford: Blackwell, 1992), pp. 74–76.

9. In "Women's Time," Julia Kristeva equates cyclical time (repetitive, according to rhythms of nature) or monumental time (eternal, timeless, mythic) to women only, although this association is not fundamentally incompatible with masculine values. The full text of "Women's Time" can be found in *The Feminist Reader: Essays in Gender and the Politics of Literary Criticism,* ed. C. Belsey and J. Moore (London: Macmillan, 1989), pp. 197–217.

10. Kristeva refers to the *chora* as a "receptacle, unnamable, improbable, hybrid, anterior to naming, to the one, to the father and consequently maternally connoted," in Julia Kristeva, *Desire in Language,* trans. Leon S. Roudiez (Oxford: Blackwell, 1980), p. 133.

# COLOR PLATES

20

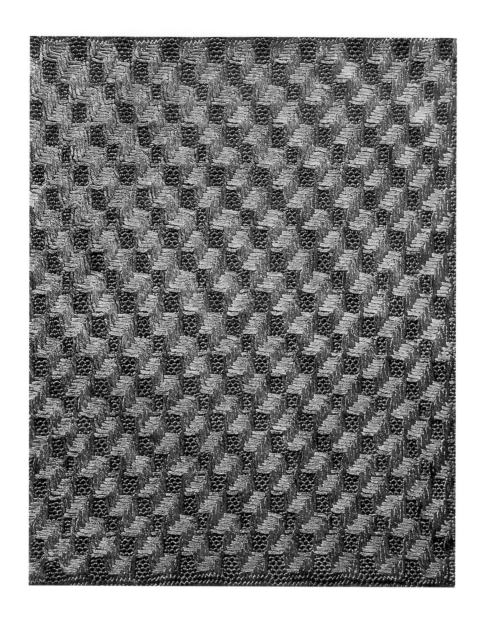

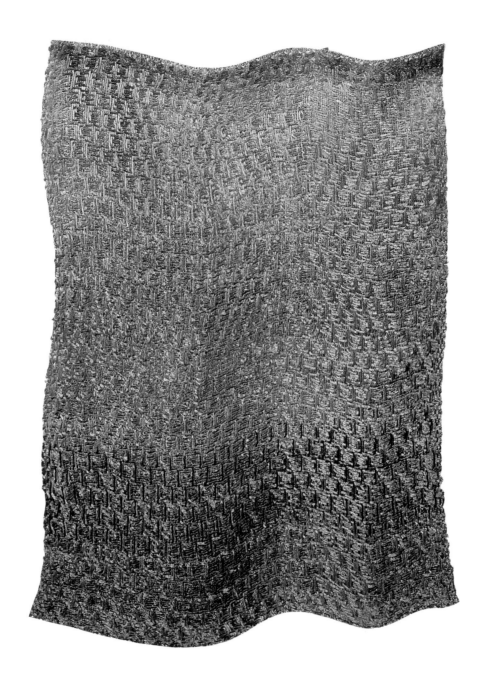

21

SHIMMER CURTAIN III, 1984

*Rayon, cotton duck, handwoven fabric; painted and pressed*

*59 ½ x 42 ½ in.*

*Collection of the Metropolitan Museum of Art, Gift of the Allrich Gallery, San Francisco, 1988*

22

PLATE 4

THROUGH THE CURTAIN AND UP FROM THE SEA, 1985
*Rayon and dye*
*48 x 40 in.*
*Collection of the artist*

24

PLATE 6

CRAZY QUILT: ROYAL REMNANTS, 1988

*Abaca, rayon, acrylic, and dye*

*62 x 49 in.*

*Collection of the artist*

PLATE 7

FRAMED AND DRAPED: MATERIAL HISTORY, 1989

*Abaca and rayon; painted and pressed*

*59 x 43 in.*

*Collection of Dr. and Mrs. Leon M. Oxman*

27

PLATE 8

TUNNEL TOO TOO, 1989

*Abaca and rayon; painted and pressed*

*53 x 43 in.*

*Collection of Joan Borinstein*

TWICE OVER, 1989
*Silk, rayon, acrylic, and dye*
*53 x 43 in.*
*Collection of the artist*

P L A T E   1 0

S H A D O W   F R I E Z E ,   1 9 9 0
*Abaca and rayon; painted and pressed*
*49 x 69 in.*
*The Saxe Collection*

PLATE 11

LEONARDO'S QUILT, 1990

*Abaca and rayon; pressed with collage*

*94 x 79 in.*

*Collection of the artist*

PLATE 12

NEW MASTER DRAPERIES: MICHELANGELO, 1991

*Abaca, rayon, acrylic, and dye*

*50 x 67 in.*

*Collection of the artist*

32

PLATE 13

NEW MASTER DRAPERIES: LEONARDO III, 1991

*Abaca, rayon, acrylic, and dye*

*73 x 50 in.*

*Collection of the artist*

33

PLATE 14

NEW MASTER DRAPERIES: LEONARDO IV, 1991

*66 x 51 in.*

*Linen, rayon, acrylic, and dye; pressed*

*Collection of Janis and William Wetsman*

34

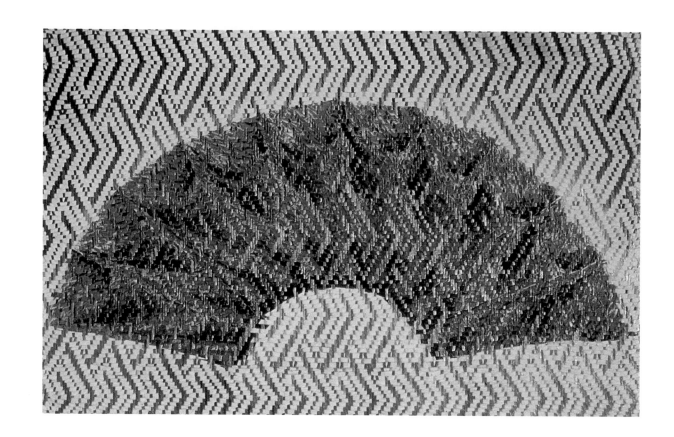

PLATE 16

LEONARDO'S FAN, 1991
*Rayon, gampi, color-Xerox transfer, and dye*
*10 x 16 in.*
*Private collection*

PLATE 17

NEW MASTER DRAPERIES: DÜRER, 1991

*Dye and acrylic on linen and rayon*

*65 x 57 in.*

*Collection of the Stephen Goldberg Family*

37

PLATE 18

NEW MASTER DRAPERIES: JACQUARD, 1992

*Silk, rayon, painted warp, and rewoven weft*

*34 x 27 in.*

*Collection of the artist*

PLATE 19

DRAPERY FRIEZE: AFTER LEONARDO, 1992

*Linen, rayon, and acrylic; dyed and pressed*

*65 x 240 in. (6 panels)*

*Collection of the artist*

40

PLATE 20

FLORENTINE FRESCO, 1992
*Linen, rayon, acrylic, and dye*
*61 x 45 ½ in.*
*Collection of Sherley Koteen*

PLATE 21

MATERIAL PLEASURES: ARTEMESIA II, 1993
*Linen, rayon, acrylic, and dye*
*63 x 52 in.*
*Collection of the artist*

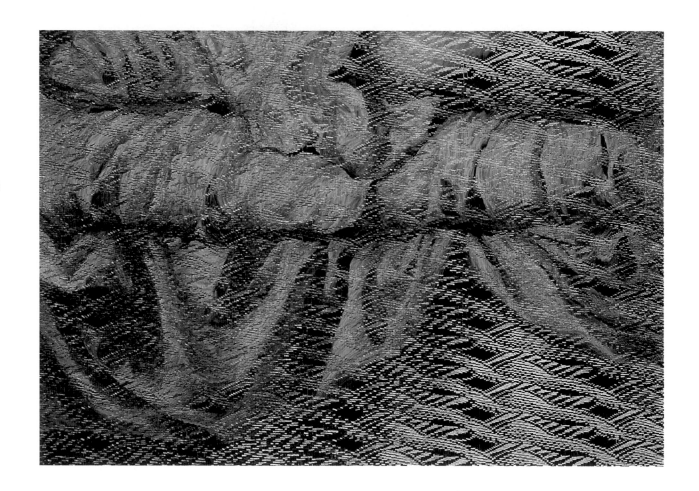

PLATE 22A

MATERIAL PLEASURES: ARTEMESIA, 1993
*From* MATERIAL PLEASURES
*Acrylic on linen, dye on rayon, and Jacquard fabric; pressed*
*53 x 76 in.*
*Collection of the artist*

43

PLATE 22B

MATERIAL PLEASURES: LEONARDO II, 1993
*From* MATERIAL PLEASURES
*Acrylic on linen, dye on rayon, and Jacquard fabric; pressed*
*65 x 53 in.*
*Collection of the artist*

PLATE 22c

TWO LOVERS, 1993
*From* MATERIAL PLEASURES
*Acrylic on linen, dye on rayon, and Jacquard fabric; pressed*
*61 x 53½ in.*
*Collection of the artist*

PLATE 23

DRAPERY FRAGMENT: MEXICO II, 1994

*Rayon, amate paper, acrylic, and dye*

*18 x 14 in.*

*Collection of the artist*

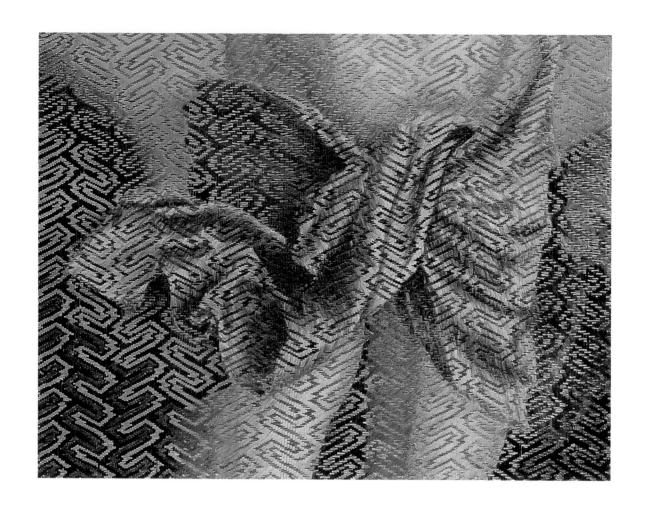

PLATE 24

LOIN CLOTH SERIES: ANONYMOUS, 1995

*Linen, rayon, acrylic, and dye*

*52 x 65 in.*

*Collection of the artist*

PLATE 25

POINT OF TOUCH: BATHSHEBA, 1995

*Linen, rayon, oil paint, and dye*

*46 x 61 in.*

*Collection of the artist*

# CHECKLIST OF THE EXHIBITION

1. *Stepping Down,* 1981
   Rayon and dye
   20 x 14 in.
   Collection of Dominic and
   Margaret Di Mare

2. *Shimmer Curtain III,* 1984
   Rayon, cotton duck, handwoven
   fabric; painted and pressed
   59½ x 42½ in.
   Collection of the Metropolitan
   Museum of Art, Gift of the Allrich
   Gallery, San Francisco, 1988

3. *Hanging Net,* 1984
   Rayon and paint
   5 x 20 x 6 in.
   Milwaukee Art Museum,
   Gift of Floyd Segel in Memory of
   Josephine Segel

4. *Through the Curtain and Up from
   the Sea,* 1985
   Rayon and dye
   48 x 40 in.
   Collection of the artist

5. *Dolly's Crazy Quilt,* 1987
   Abaca and rayon; painted
   and pressed
   62 x 57 in.
   Collection of the Oakland
   Museum of California, 87.35

6. *Crazy Quilt: Royal Remnants,* 1988
   Abaca, rayon, acrylic, and dye
   62 x 49 in.
   Collection of the artist

7. *Framed and Draped:
   Material History,* 1989
   Abaca and rayon; painted
   and pressed
   59 x 43 in.
   Collection of Dr. and Mrs.
   Leon M. Oxman

8. *Tunnel Too Too,* 1989
   Abaca and rayon; painted
   and pressed
   53 x 43 in.
   Collection of Joan Borinstein

9. *Twice Over,* 1989
   Silk, rayon, acrylic, and dye
   53 x 43 in.
   Collection of the artist

10. *Shadow Frieze,* 1990
    Abaca and rayon; painted
    and pressed
    49 x 69 in.
    The Saxe Collection

11. *Leonardo's Quilt,* 1990
    Abaca and rayon; pressed
    with collage
    94 x 79 in.
    Collection of the artist

12. *New Master Draperies:
    Michelangelo,* 1991
    Abaca, rayon, acrylic, and dye
    50 x 67 in.
    Collection of the artist

13. *New Master Draperies:
    Leonardo III,* 1991
    Abaca, rayon, acrylic, and dye
    73 x 50 in.
    Collection of the artist

14. *New Master Draperies:*
    *Leonardo IV,* 1991
    Linen, rayon, acrylic, and dye;
    pressed
    66 x 51 in.
    Collection of Janis and William
    Wetsman

15. *Drapery Fan,* 1991
    Rayon, gampi, color-Xerox
    transfer, and dye
    10 x 15 in.
    Private collection

16. *Leonardo's Fan,* 1991
    Rayon, gampi, color-Xerox
    transfer, and dye
    10 x 16 in.
    Private collection

17. *New Master Draperies: Dürer,* 1991
    Dye and acrylic on linen and rayon
    65 x 57 in.
    Collection of the Stephen Goldberg
    Family

18. *New Master Draperies: Jacquard,*
    1992
    Silk, rayon, painted warp, and
    rewoven weft
    34 x 27 in.
    Collection of the artist

19. *Drapery Frieze: After Leonardo,* 1992
    Linen, rayon, and acrylic; dyed
    and pressed
    65 x 240 in. (6 panels)
    Collection of the artist

20. *Florentine Fresco,* 1992
    Linen, rayon, acrylic, and dye
    61 x 45½ in.
    Collection of Sherley Koteen

21. *Material Pleasures: Artemesia II,*
    1993
    Linen, rayon, acrylic, and dye
    63 x 52 in.
    Collection of the artist

22. *Material Pleasures,* 1993
    *Material Pleasures: Leonardo I*
    *Material Pleasures: Leonardo II*
    *Material Pleasures: Dürer*
    *Material Pleasures: Artemesia*
    *Material Pleasures: Giulio R.*
    *Two Lovers*
    Acrylic on linen, dye on rayon, and
    Jacquard fabric; pressed
    16 x 32 ft. (suggested installation)
    Collection of the artist

23. *Drapery Fragment: Mexico II,* 1994
    Rayon, amate paper, acrylic,
    and dye
    18 x 14 in.
    Collection of the artist

24. *Loin Cloth Series: Anonymous,* 1995
    Linen, rayon, acrylic and dye
    52 x 65 in.
    Collection of the artist

25. *Point of Touch: Bathsheba,* 1995
    Linen, rayon, oil paint, and dye
    46 x 61 in.
    Collection of the artist

# CHRONOLOGY

## 1942
Born in Ventura, California, to James Paul and Esther Miriam Holman Polese. Moves with family to San Francisco Bay Area.

## 1946—48
Family lives with grandmother Esther G. Holman, in Berkeley. Influenced by grandmother's tales of travel to Europe, the Middle East, and the Pacific, and by the collection of photographs and artifacts from Germany and the Philippines, where her grandparents had lived before the First World War.

## 1956—60
Student at Menlo Atherton High School, where she focuses on theater; enrolls in special summer theater program at San Francisco State University.

## 1960—65
Studies theater at San Francisco State University. Studies painting, ceramics, and political science at University of California, Berkeley; bachelor of arts degree in political science.

## 1965
Travels to Mexico for two months; first exposure to process of weaving. Collects textiles, especially from Oaxaca and Chiapas.

## 1966
Returns to University of California, Berkeley, for postgraduate courses in education and art. Teaches in the Richmond public schools.

## 1967
Marries first husband, David Cook, an artist. Travels with him to Sweden.

## 1967—68
Studies weaving in Sweden and travels extensively in Western Europe and Soviet Union. Absorbs as much historic and contemporary art as possible. Particularly influenced by visits to *Documenta 4* in Kassel and the Biennale in Venice.

## 1968
Returns to Berkeley and joins an energetic and experimental art community, which emphasizes breaking media boundaries, using nontraditional materials and forms. Begins to develop unique style, combining strong technical background in weaving with painting, dyeing, printmaking, photography, and the study of historic and ethnic textiles.

## 1968—71
Works independently. Takes summer courses at University of California, Berkeley, in textiles. Studies photographic techniques, dyeing, and printing independently. Joins group of women artists committed to sharing professional experiences, research, and material resources; group continues meeting well into the 1970s and serves as an important conduit for contemporary fiber activities in the Bay Area and throughout the United States.

## 1971—73
Studies with Ed Rossbach at University of California, Berkeley; he remains both a friend and an important influence on her work and thought. Earns master of arts degree in design.

**1973**

Develops technique used to create undulating *Fabric Landscape* works. Exhibits in the 6th International Biennial of Tapestry, Musée Cantonal des Beaux-Arts, Lausanne; work is well received. Meets many European, Japanese, and American fiber artists. Meets Mildred Constantine, curator and writer, and Jack Larsen, of Larsen Inc., textile designer and writer. Included in *Anatomy and Fabric,* an exhibition at the Los Angeles County Museum of Art. Starts teaching at University of California, Davis, Department of Design.

**1974**

Receives first National Endowment for the Arts fellowship (others in 1977, 1986, and 1992). Begins career-long association with Louise Allrich of the Allrich Gallery, San Francisco. Receives commission from architect John Portman to create three-story tapestry for the Embarcadero Center, San Francisco. Starts series of works using direct photographic process on relief-woven surfaces. Participates in the development of Fiberworks, School of the Textile Arts, where she serves on the advisory board until 1979.

**1975**

Exhibits large-scale, dimensional *Space-Dyed Photographic Weaving*, exploring detail, image, and structure, in the 7th International Biennial of Tapestry, Musée Cantonal des Beaux-Arts, Lausanne. Begins showing at Hadler Rodrigues Gallery, in New York.

**1976**

Birth of son, Kalle Cook. Joins faculty of the California College of Arts and Crafts in Oakland, where she has remained; currently professor of art. Completes one of the first United States Government GSA commissions, for the Social Security Building in Richmond, California.

**1977**

Participates in the exhibition *Fiberworks: Japan and the Americas,* at the National Museums of Modern Art in Kyoto and Tokyo. Exhibits in the 8th International Biennial of Tapestry, Musée Cantonal des Beaux-Arts, Lausanne.

**1978**

First major solo exhibition at the Allrich Gallery. Exhibits by invitation in Triennale of Tapestry, Centralne Muzeum Włókiennictwa, Lodz, Poland.

**1980**

First solo museum exhibition, San Jose Museum of Art. Two-person exhibition at the Renwick Gallery, National Museum of American Art, Washington, D.C., with Neda El Hilali; first shows "woven canvases" (industrial rayon, compressed wet under pressure, hammered, and painted).

**1981**

Work featured in the book *Beyond Craft: The Art of Fabric,* written by Mildred Constantine and Jack Larsen. Shows in traveling exhibition by the same name. Creates *Spear* series. Receives National Endowment for the Arts special projects grant for study of early Jacquard techniques; travels to England and France. Begins experimental work with Jacquard loom. Participates in Jacquard Project at Rhode Island School of Design. American Craft Museum, New York, acquires *Emergence,* a work from the *Fabric Landscape* series. Separates from husband; divorce follows.

1982
ABC Television features one-half-hour interview with Cook in "Handmade in America: Conversations with Fourteen Craftmasters." The Museum of Modern Art, New York, acquires *Transposition II.* Sees exhibition *Leonardo's Return to Vinci,* which includes some of his drapery studies, at the University Art Museum, Berkeley; these studies become an important influence on her later *New Master Draperies* series.

1983
French government sponsors a solo exhibition, with a catalogue documenting all work to date, at the Galerie Nationale de la Tapisserie et d'Art Textile, Beauvais. Early fabric image work, *Fabric II,* is purchased for Fond National d'Art Contemporain (the French national collection). Marries second husband, Mark Delepine, an educator.

1984
Creates *Curtain* pieces, which use textiles as both object and subject matter; work is woven on the loom, distorted, and pressed to hold form and illusion of motion. Exhibits *Shimmer Curtains* and *Stage Curtains* at the Allrich Gallery. Travels to China as part of United States Textile Delegation. Trip influences new, colorful curtain series, *China Stage Curtains.*

1987
Invited by the city of Kyoto to be part of an international jury for the First International Textile Competition in Kyoto. Travels to Japan twice; collects new materials and observes traditional Japanese textile-making techniques. First shows *Crazy Quilts* as part of exhibition of domestic textile objects—kitchen curtains, towels, pockets, and imitation quilts—at the Allrich Gallery. *Dolly's Crazy Quilt,* inspired by a quilt made by her native Californian great-grandmother, Dolly (Kathryn Boyes Hopkins), in 1889, acquired by The Oakland Museum. Becomes an honorary board member of the James Renwick Alliance in Washington, D.C.

1988
*Shimmer Curtain III* acquired by the Metropolitan Museum of Art, New York.

1989
Receives Excellence Award in International Textile Competition '89, Kyoto, for *Sashay,* the first in a series of new works using the glazed, painted images of fabric as subject matter. *Sashay* subsequently acquired by Det Danske Kunstindustrimuseum (Museum of Decorative Arts) in Copenhagen.

1990
Writes essay on Ed Rossbach for the book *Ed Rossbach: 40 Years of Exploration and Innovation in Fiber Art.* Honored with solo exhibition at the National Academy of Sciences in Washington, D.C. Learns ancient silk-weaving techniques on the hand Jacquard loom as an invited artist-in-residence at the Fondazione Arte della Seta Lissio, Florence. Researches drapery images in Italian Renaissance paintings in Venice, Florence, and Lucca. Awarded California Arts Council artist fellowship grant.

1991
Creates painted, woven works, *New Master Draperies,* inspired by drapery studies by the old masters; first pieces that connect fabric to presence of the human body under the cloth. Exhibits *New Master Draperies* at Bellas Artes Gallery, New York. Participates in International Jacquard Project, sponsored by the Müller-Zell Company, Zell, Germany; creates three-dimensional drapery *Drape on Drape on Drape,* combining computer Jacquard images of drapery with roller-screen-printed warp and installation. *Crazy Too Quilt* acquired by Renwick Gallery, National Museum of American Art, Washington, D.C.

**1 9 9 3**

Solo exhibition at Ram Gallery, Oslo. Invited to do installation
*Material Pleasures* at the Museum Van Bommel-Van Dam in
Venlo, the Netherlands, the first large work in a new series
emphasizing the "point of touch" between cloth and the body.
Awarded the United States/Mexico Creative Artist's Resi-
dency; spends two months in Mexico City hosted by Mexican
government and Bellas Artes (national arts organization of
Mexico). Creates work influenced by Mexican indigenous
textiles and Mexican historical painting.

**1 9 9 4**

Awarded French Fellowship by the National Endowment for
the Arts; spends six months in Paris, at Cité Internationale des
Arts. Researches drapery and fabric images in paintings at the
Louvre and other museums throughout France. Continues
work concerned with fabric and the body, developing both the
*Loin Cloth* series and the *Point of Touch* series. Lectures at Royal
College of Art and Goldsmiths, London.

**1 9 9 5**

Included in exhibition *Conceptual Textiles,* organized by the
Kohler Art Museum, Sheboygan, Wisconsin. *Lia Cook: Material
Allusions,* solo exhibition organized by the Oakland Museum of
California.

# Selected Bibliography

Berman, Susan. "The Rise of the Fiber People." *California Living, San Francisco Examiner and Chronicle,* July 14, 1974.

Colchester, Chloe. *The New Textiles: Trends and Traditions.* London: Thames and Hudson, 1991.

Cook, Lia. "Swatches." *Fiberarts* 21, no. 5 (March–April 1995): 13.

_____. "Emerging West Coast Artists." *Fiberarts* 19, no. 4 (January–February 1993): 36–44.

_____. "Fiber National 1991 Juror's Statement." *Fiber National 1991.* Exh. cat. Dunkirk, N.Y.: Adams Art Gallery, 1991.

_____. "Ed Rossbach as Educator: A Personal View." In *Ed Rossbach: 40 Years of Exploration and Innovation in Fiber Art.* Edited by Anne Pollard Rowe and Rebecca A. T. Stevens. Asheville, N.C.: Lark Books; Washington, D.C.: The Textile Museum, 1990.

Conner, Maureen. "The Tapestries of Lia Cook." *Arts Magazine* 59, no. 6 (February 1985): 94–95.

Constantine, Mildred, and Jack Larsen. *Beyond Craft: The Art of Fabric.* New York: Van Nostrand Reinhold, 1981.

Diamonstein, Barbaralee. *Handmade in America: Conversations with Fourteen Craftmasters.* New York: Harry N. Abrams, 1984.

Frankenstein, Alfred. "Puttering around and Creating." *San Francisco Chronicle,* May 25, 1978.

Fukunaga, Shigeki. *Fiberworks: Japan and the Americas.* Exh. cat. Kyoto: National Museum of Modern Art, 1977.

Hall, Julie. *Traditions and Change: The New American Craftsman.* New York: E. P. Dutton, 1978.

Held, Shirley E. *Weaving: A Handbook of the Fiber Arts.* New York: Holt, Reinhardt and Winston, 1978.

Janeiro, Jan. "Lia Cook: On the Loom of Contradiction." *American Craft* 40 (June–July 1980): 28–31.

_____. "Textiles about Textiles." *Fiberarts* 18, no. 5 (March–April 1992): 52–56.

Kinsella, Patricia. "The Jacquard Project." *Weaver's* 15, no. 4 (1991): 32–35.

Larsen, Jack. *Interlace.* Tokyo: Kodansha International, 1987.

_____. *The Dyer's Art.* New York: Van Nostrand Reinhold, 1976.

Margetts, Martina. *International Crafts.* London: Thames and Hudson, 1991.

O'Hara, Sheila. "Art and Industry: The Jacquard Project." *Shuttle, Spindle & Dyepot* 23, no. 1 (Winter 1991–92): 44–46.

Rowley, Kathleen. "Lia Cook: Shaped and Woven Constructions." *Fiberarts* 12, no. 1 (July–August 1985): 66.

Scarborough, Jessica. "From a Gallery Owner's Perspective: An Interview with Louise Allrich." *Fiberarts* 21, no. 1 (Summer 1994): 42–45.

Scheinman, Pamela. "New Ends: The Medium as Message." *Fiberarts* 18, no. 3 (November–December 1991): 65–66.

_____. "Reviews: Textiles about Textiles." *Fiberarts* 21, no. 3 (November–December 1994): 60–61.

Schira, Cynthia. "Kyoto '89 International Textile Competition." *Surface Design Journal* 14, no. 4 (Summer 1990): 10–13.

56     \_\_\_\_\_. "The Jacquard Project." *American Craft* 52 (February–March 1992): 38–41.

\_\_\_\_\_. "The Jacquard Project: A Revolution in Weaving." *Fiberarts* 18, no. 5 (March–April 1992): 12–13.

Sheenhan, Dianne. *Ideas in Weaving.* Loveland: Interweave Press, 1989.

Talley, Charles S. "The Woven Paintings of Lia Cook." *Vav Magasinet / Scandinavian Weaving Magazine,* no. 3 (1986): 4–6.

\_\_\_\_\_. "Seductive Threads." *Artweek* 20, no. 13 (April 1, 1989): 6.

Thomas, Michel. *Textile Art.* New York: Rizzoli International Publications, 1985.

Tryba, Mildred. "Surface Design in Fiber R/Evolution." *Surface Design Journal* 10, no. 4 (Summer 1986): 12–13.

Van Gelder, Lydia. *Ikat.* New York: Watson-Guptill, 1980.

Werther, Betty. "The 14th International Biennial of Tapestry." *American Craft* 49 (October–November 1989): 54–59.

Westphal, Katherine, and Ed Rossbach. "Filaments of the Imagination." *American Craft* 41 (June–July 1981): 10–15.